Windows Server 2008 R2

Interview Questions

You'll Most Likely Be Asked

Job Interview Questions Series

VP Vibrant Publishers

www.vibrantpublishers.com

Windows Server 2008 R2
Interview Questions You'll Most Likely Be Asked

ISBN-10: 147518834X
ISBN-13: 9781475188349

Library of Congress Control Number: 2012906685

This publication is designed to provide accurate and authoritative information in regard to the subject matter covered. The author has made every effort in the preparation of this book to ensure the accuracy of the information. However, information in this book is sold without warranty either expressed or implied. The Author or the Publisher will not be liable for any damages caused or alleged to be caused either directly or indirectly by this book.

Vibrant Publishers books are available at special quantity discount for sales promotions, or for use in corporate training programs. For more information please write to **bulkorders@vibrantpublishers.com**

Please email feedback / corrections (technical, grammatical or spelling) to **spellerrors@vibrantpublishers.com**

To access the complete catalogue of Vibrant Publishers, visit **www.vibrantpublishers.com**

Table of Contents

This page is intentionally left blank

Windows Server 2008 R2

Review these typical interview questions and think about how you would answer them. Read the answers listed; you will find best possible answers along with strategies and suggestions.

This page is intentionally left blank

Basics of Windows Server 2008 R2

1: What is static routing?

Answer:

When administrators manually edit and add the IP addresses of next routers (hops) in the routing table of servers the packets get transferred to those particular interfaces only. This manual specification of the next hops is called static routing.

2: What is dynamic routing?

Answer:

When entries in routing table are managed through protocols such as Routing Information Protocol (RIP) or Open Shortest Path First (OSPF) the process is known as dynamic routing. When dynamic routing is configured, routers automatically choose best path to forward packets to their destinations.

3: What do you understand by NAT?

Answer:

Network Address Translation or NAT is the process through which, in most cases, a single public IP address is shared among multiple computers on a local area network that have been assigned with the private IP addresses by the administrators.

4: What is OSI reference model?

Answer:

The Open System Interconnection (OSI) reference model was first developed by the International Standard Organizations in early 1980's. It was designed to allow communication between two computers efficiently and in a secure way. The OSI reference model defines the process of how data should be transferred between two networking devices of different vendors. According to OSI reference model, data that is transferred between two computers or networking devices is manipulated on all its seven layers accordingly.

5: How many layers does OSI reference model contain?

Answer:

OSI reference model has seven layers in all, namely:

a) Physical Layer

b) Data Link Layer

c) Network Layer

d) Transport Layer

e) Session Layer

f) Presentation Layer

g) Application Layer

6: What is the difference between TCP and UDP?

Answer:

TCP stands for Transmission Control Protocol and is connection oriented which means that it verifies if the destination computer is connected before it starts sending the packets.

UDP or User Datagram Protocol on the other hand is connectionless protocol that sends packets to the destination computer without checking the connection state.

7: How many layers does TCP/IP Protocol Stack contain?

Answer:

TCP/IP Protocol Stack contains fout layers, namely Application, Transport, Internet and Network.

8: Routers function at which layer of OSI reference model?

Answer:

Since routers mostly deal with IP addresses, they function at third layer of OSI reference model.

9: What are routing protocols?

Answer:

Routing protocols are the protocols that help routers communicate with each other and share their routing tables.

10: What are port numbers?

Answer:

Port numbers are the logical gates identified by numeric characters. These logical gates are used when a computer receives or sends information. Because of port numbers computers accept or deny the packets depending on the configuration in the firewalls or routers. For example if an administrator has blocked port number 23 on a router, it cannot accept telnet requests whatsoever.

11: Name the types of wireless topologies.

Answer:

There are two wireless topologies that can be used while

establishing WLAN infrastructure, namely Ad-hoc and Infrastructure.

12 What do you understand by the term VLAN?

Answer:

VLAN or Virtual LAN is a term and configuration mostly used in Cisco platforms. With the help of VLAN, a managed LAN switch is divided into multiple logical switches. Technically every LAN port of a switch has its own broadcast domain. VLANS are mostly configured in large production environment and where multiple subnets are deployed by the administrators.

13: What is the difference between network and subnet?

Answer:

Network can be considered a container for single or multiple subnets of different IP address ranges whereas a subnet is a part of a network that has a specific IP address range. For example a network may have an IP address 192.168.0.0/26 and 192.168.0.0 - 192.168.0.63/26 is a subnet in the network.

14: What is the major difference between Tracert and Pathping command?

Answer:

Tracert is a tool that is used to determine the route of the packets. It only gives the information about the routers (hops) through which the packet passes to reach its destination. On the other hand, Pathping not only traces the route but also shows the time taken by the packets sent to each hop (router), hence checking the connection state as well. It gives complete information about the number of packets which are dropped and also about the packets that successfully reached their destinations.

15: What is the difference between Multicast and Broadcast?
Answer:
Multicast is the process in which a message is transmitted to a group or set of computers whereas in Broadcast the message is transmitted to all computers.

16: Which protocol does IPv4 use to resolve broadcast addresses into Media Access Control (MAC) addresses of NICs?
Answer:
Address Resolution Protocol (ARP) is used to resolve broadcast addresses into MAC addresses.

Active Directory Services
Installation and
Administration

17: You want to promote one of your Windows Server 2008 R2 machine as a Domain Controller. Which command you will type to do so?

Answer:

You can initiate this process by adding the Active Directory Domain Services server role to the server and then you can execute DCPromo command. Alternatively you can type DCPROMO.EXE command directly in the Run command box to kick start AD DS installation wizard.

18: Which command would you use to add or remove roles in Windows Server 2008 R2 Server Core?

Answer:

Ocsetup.exe command is used to add or remove roles in Windows Server 2008 R2 Server Core Edition except for Active Directory Domain Services (AD DS), which is added by using Dcpromo.exe command.

19: You are the Administrator of a company named DATACORP.COM. It contains Windows Server 2008 R2 promoted as a Domain Controller and configured as Global Catalog (GC) which also holds all five operation master roles. You have also deployed another Domain Controller in your domain. However, it is not configured as GC. What Flexible Single Master Operations (FSMO) Role should you transfer to the non-GC domain controller?

Answer:

Infrastructure Master Role must be transferred to the non-GC

domain controller. This step is mandatory because if Infrastructure Master and Global Catalog remain on the same server, Infrastructure Master would not update NTDS.dit file when GC updates itself. This role transfer step is not necessary if there is only one Domain Controller in the network.

20: What are the pre-requisites to add a computer to the domain?

Answer:

A computer must have physical connection to the network, it must have IP address and appropriate DNS address assigned to it, user who wishes to add the computer to a domain must have administrative privileges on the local computer and must have any domain user account credentials for domain authentication while adding.

21: What is pre-staging?

Answer:

Pre-staging means a computer account is manually created in a domain before the client computer is actually added to it. This helps administrators place computer accounts in the desired OU and apply appropriate group policies on them.

22: How many types of Operation Master Roles are there in a forest?

Answer:

There are five Operation Master Roles in an Active Directory forest and are divided in two main categories.

a) **Forest Wide Roles:**

    i.   **Schema Master:** Schema Master is responsible for the changes that are made to the schema of the forest.

    ii.   **Domain Naming Master:** Domain Naming Master is responsible for adding or removing domains in the forest. It also checks if any domain name already exists in the forest while creating a new domain.

b) **Domain Wide Roles:**

    i.   **PDC Emulator:** Primary Domain Controller (PDC) Emulator is responsible for password updates, time synchronization and manages Group Policy updates within a Domain.

    ii.   **RID Master:** RID (Relative ID) Master is responsible for issuing Security Identifiers (SIDs) for the objects in the domain. SIDs are issued by RID Master in the lot of 500.

    iii.   **Infrastructure Master:** Infrastructure Master maintains the records of modifications of the groups or users of other domains in the forest.

23: How many types of Active Directory partitions are there?

Answer:

Active Directory has four partitions namely:

a) **Domain Partition:** Contains information about all the domain objects including Users, Groups, Published Folders, etc.

b) **Schema Partition:** It maintains records for all attributes

of all object classes forestwide.

c) **Application Directory Partition:** Creates and manages active directory replication topologies. It also maintains records for DNS replication scopes.

d) **Configuration Partition:** Maintains and manages the logical structure of the forests. Logical structure may include structures of domains, etc. Configuration partition also contains information about physical structure such as subnets, sites, etc.

24: In which case you should enable Universal Group Membership Caching (UGMC) in a site?
Answer:

When a domain or forest is expanded at distant geographical locations multiple sites are created and configured accordingly. It is recommended that Global Catalog server must be present in every site but sometimes if the two branches are connected to each other via slow WAN link, synchronization between two Global Catalog servers consumes a decent amount of time and Internet bandwidth. To avoid such situations Universal Group Membership Caching should be enabled on the servers located at branch offices which can then cache the information of Global Catalog server present in the main branch.

25: How many Forest Functional Levels does Windows Server 2008 R2 have?
Answer:

Windows Server 2008 R2 has four Forest Functional Levels as

written below:

a) **Windows 2000:** This FFL must be configured on Windows Server 2008 R2 if the forest contains Domain Controllers that run Windows 2000 Servers, Windows Server 2003, Windows Server 2008 and Windows Server 2008 R2.

b) **Windows Server 2003:** This FFL must be configured if Windows Server 2008 R2 domain controller is to be installed in the forest that already has domain controllers that run Windows Server 2003, Windows Server 2008 and Windows Server 2008 R2 operating systems.

c) **Windows Server 2008:** This FFL can be configured when the forest has existing Windows Server 2008 and Windows Server 2008 R2 domain controllers.

d) **Windows Server 2008 R2:** This FFL can be used if the forest has existing Windows Server 2008 R2 domain controllers only. This can also be configured if administrators plan to use Windows Server 2008 R2 operating systems only for future expansions.

26: Which Operation Master role is responsible for time synchronization and password changing?

Answer:

PDC Emulator is the Operation Master Role in Windows Server 2008 R2 Active Directory infrastructure that is responsible for time synchronization and password changes.

27: What do you understand by the term Certificate Revocation?

Answer:

Certificate Revocation is when a certificate is either expired or is revoked manually by the administrators because of inappropriate acts initiated by the users. When a certificate is revoked its information is updated in Certificate Revocation List or CRL.

28: What is the function of Infrastructure Master Role?

Answer:

Infrastructure Master regularly communicates with Global Catalog server on the network and updates itself with the latest partial information of the objects located in other domains. If there are multiple domain controllers present in a network, server holding Infrastructure Master role must not be the same computer that is also a Global Catalog server.

29: What is symmetric encryption?

Answer:

Symmetric encryption is the encryption method where same encryption key is used to encrypt and decrypt data.

30: What is Asymmetric encryption?

Answer:

Asymmetric encryption is the process of encryption where a key pair is used to encrypt or decrypt data. In asymmetric encryption type public and private keys are used for encryption and decryption and information encrypted using public key can only be decrypted using the corresponding private key and vice versa.

31: What do you understand by single sign on (SSO)?
Answer:

Single Sign On or SSO is a feature that administrators use to allow users to access objects on different domains or forests without providing credentials every time they access them. Active Directory Federation Services or AD FS must be installed to configure SSO. Example may include some sites that also allow users to logon using Facebook credentials.

32: What do you understand by Network Device Enrollment Service (NDES)?
Answer:

Network Device Enrollment Service is a service through which Routers and Switches can also be a part of Public Key Infrastructure (PKI). It uses a protocol known as Simple Certificate Enrollment Protocol (SCEP) developed by Cisco which helps devices and users to auto-enroll digital certificates for authentication purposes.

33: What is the difference between trusted domain and trusting domain?
Answer:

A trusting domain is the one that allows users from trusted domains to access its objects whereas trusted domains are the ones users of which are allowed to access the objects that reside in trusting domains. By default two-way trust is automatically established between the two domains that reside in a single Active Directory forest.

34: What is a pre-shared key?

Answer:

Pre-shared key is a numeric and alphanumeric key combination that is stored in clear text (unencrypted format) and is used to pair or authenticate two devices before actual communication takes place between them. In most production environments use of pre-shared key is not at all recommended however it can be used for testing purposes.

35: What is Integrated Windows Authentication?

Answer:

Integrated Windows Authentication is a process through which Microsoft products use Windows user accounts to allow access to the users. Integrated Windows Authentication is mostly used in IIS where credentials of active directory user accounts are used.

36: What are bridgehead servers?

Answer:

A Bridgehead server is a dedicated domain controller in every site that communicates with the bridgehead server of other site for active directory replication.

37: What is the function of Key Recovery Agent (KRA)?

Answer:

While encrypting files or folders encryption keys are used. Encryption keys are also used to decrypt files or folders when users need access to them. If because of any reason encryption keys are lost encrypted files or folders become permanently inaccessible. To avoid these situations Key Recovery Agents or KRAs are configured which are capable of recovering the lost encryption keys.

38: What is Client Certificate Authentication method?

Answer:

Client Certificate Authentication is a method that enables Web-based Client computers to verify themselves on the Web servers. In this method client computers are authenticated by the Web server through the security certificate installed on them. Certificates are issued to the client computers either by local or third-party trusted Certificate Authorities (CAs), e.g. VeriSign.

39: What is Selective Authentication?

Answer:

Selective Authentication is the feature in Windows Server 2008 R2 which, when enabled, allows administrators to specify which user accounts are authorized to access shared resources from other forests while establishing trust relationships between them.

40: What is a trust?

Answer:

In an active directory forest, trust is when two domains or forests allow users from other domains or forests to access their objects. In an active directory forest, if there are multiple domains, a two-way trust is automatically established between the domains. If an organization has multiple forests, administrators must manually establish trusts between them.

41: What are the prerequisites for deploying AD FS (Active Directory Federation Services)?

Answer:

Each participating active directory forest must have the following prerequisites for deploying AD FS:

a) Domain Controller = 1
b) Member server hosting internal AD FS = 1
c) Member server hosting AD FS proxy server = 1
d) Microsoft SQL Server 2005 = 1

42: What is the use of Active Directory Recycle Bin in Windows Server 2008 R2?

Answer:

Active Directory Recycle Bin is the new feature in Windows Server 2008 R2. It allows administrators to recover Active Directory objects when they are deleted accidently.

43: What is Distinguished Name?

Answer:

Distinguished Name is a combination of strings and attributes, mainly used by LDAP for recognizing LDAP objects. It is a sequence of Relative Distinguished Names (RDN), which is separated by commas. An e.g. of Distinguished Name is-

DN = CN=John,OU=Sales,DC=Abc,DC=Com

where CN=John, OU=Sales, DC=Abc and DC=Com are individual RDNs for above DN.

44: What is Auto Enrollment?

Answer:

Auto Enrollment is a process by which computers and users automatically enroll themselves for certificates and smart cards. Auto Enrollment can be configured through group policy.

45: What are the two types of Replication Transport Protocols in Active Directory Sites and Services snap-in?

Answer:

Directory Service Remote Procedure Call (DS-RPC): DS-RPC is used for Intrasite and Intersite Replication and it appears as IP sub-container under Inter-Site Transports container in Active Directory Sites and Services snap-in.

Inter-Site Messaging-Simple Mail Transfer Protocol (ISM-SMTP): ISM-SMTP is used for intersite messaging.

46: What is a Global Catalog Server?

Answer:

A Global Catalog Server contains partial information and/or

replica of every active directory object in every domain in a forest.

47: What is the function of Schema Master?

Answer:

Schema Master Role is responsible for the changes in schema in a Forest. It controls and maintains all modification and updates to the schema. An example may be the additional attribute for e-mail address that becomes available once Exchange Server is installed in an Active Directory forest.

48: Which protocol is used by AD LDS?

Answer:

Lightweight Directory Access Protocol (LDAP) is used by AD LDS that works on port TCP 389.

49: What are the core elements of the AD CS infrastructure?

Answer:

AD CS is made up of four core elements:
  a) **Certificate Authorities:** Dedicated servers to generate and issue digital certificates to users and/or devices
  b) **CA Web Enrollment:** Allows certificate enrollment processes using web interface
  c) **Online Responders:** Maintains the records of the current status of digital certificates
  d) **Network Device Enrollment Service:** Generates certificates for network devices such as LAN switches or routers. It also enrolls and authenticates the devices

and helps them in communicating with the network

50: What is Certificate Revocation List (CRL)?

Answer:

Certificate Revocation List is a list of certificates that are cancelled or revoked by the issuing authority.

51: Describe the concept of Administrator role separation.

Answer:

Administrator role separation feature helps administrators grant local administrative privileges to non-administrator user accounts. By delegating local administrative tasks to specific users or groups, administrators can grant them the ability to log on to the server, update drivers and restart the servers. However such users cannot manage Active Directory or Directory Services.

52: Which FSMO roles you can transfer from a domain controller to another domain controller in a different domain in a forest?

Answer:

Schema Master Role and Domain Naming Master Role.

53: In which condition you can replicate SYSVOL by using DFS-R within that domain?

Answer:

DFS-R can be used to replicate SYSVOL only when the Domain Functional Level is Windows Server 2008 or higher.

54: What is Intersite replication?

Answer:

When replication takes place between two sites, this type of replication is known as Intersite replication. An example may be replication that may occur between two branch offices of a company which may be expanded in two different countries.

55: What is Intrasite replication?

Answer:

When replication takes place between two domain controllers that reside in a common site, this type of replication is known as Intrasite replication.

56: What should be the minimum Forest and Domain Functional Level for deploying RODC?

Answer:

We can deploy Read Only Domain Controllers (RODC) in a network where Forest and Domain Functional Level is Windows Server 2003 or higher.

57: Name the built-in Data Collector Sets in Windows Server 2008 R2.

Answer:

Built-in Data Collector Sets in Windows Server 2008 R2 are Active Directory Diagnostics, LAN Diagnostics, System Diagnostics, System Performance and Wireless Diagnostics.

58: What is Data Collector Set?

Answer:

Data Collector Sets are used to collect system information. The information includes configuration settings and performance data. It stores collected data in a file which can be later viewed in performance monitor.

59: What is the difference between Enterprise CA and Standalone CA?

Answer:

Enterprise CA can be integrated only in Domain Controllers whereas Standalone CA can be deployed only in a member server or in a standalone server (a server which is not the part of a domain). Enterprise CAs can run only on Windows Server 2008 R2 Enterprise Edition and Datacenter Edition. On the other hand, Standalone CAs can be configured on Windows Server 2008 R2 Standard Edition as well.

60: Which Server Roles are supported by Windows Server 2008 R2 Server Core?

Answer:

Following roles are supported by a server running Windows Server 2008 R2 Server Core:

a) Active Directory Domain Services

b) Active Directory Certificate Services

c) Active Directory Lightweight Directory Services

d) Internet Information Service Server (IIS) or Web Server (which also includes a subset of ASP.NET)

e) Print and Document Services

f) File Services (which also includes File Resource Manager)

g) DNS Server

h) DHCP Server

i) Hyper-V

j) Media Streaming Services

61: What do you understand by RODC credential caching?

Answer:

Read Only Domain Controller Credential Caching is a process in which credentials of domain user accounts are locally cached on the RODC. Because of this process credentials of user accounts are not sent to the read/write domain controllers which, in many cases, may be located at geographically distant locations and connected to the branch offices via slow WAN links. This process remarkably reduces the consumption of Internet bandwidth.

62: Where does Active Directory store its Database?

Answer:

Active directory stores its database in a file called NTDS.dit which is located at %systemroot%\System32\NTDS.

63: What do you understand by the process Offline Domain Join?

Answer:

Offline Domain Join is the process, which is newly added in Windows Server 2008 R2. Because of this feature computers running Windows 7 and/or Windows Server 2008 R2 can be added to a domain without having network connectivity with the domain controller.

64: What are Site Link Bridges?

Answer:

Site Link Bridges are connection types that connect two or more sites by creating transitivity between them. For example, if site A connects to site B and site B connects to site C using Site Link Bridges, then site A automatically connects to site C for Active Directory replication.

65: Describe the features provided by Windows Server2008 R2 domain functional level.

Answer:

New Windows Server 2008 R2 Forest and Domain Functional level features are:

a) AD Administrative Center is a new interface for administrative tasks

b) Active Directory module for Windows PowerShell and Windows PowerShell cmdlets

c) Active Directory Recycle Bin to store accidently deleted Active Directory objects

d) Managed Service Accounts

e) Offline Domain Join

f) Authentication Assurance for Active Directory Federation Services (AD FS)

66: How can you create application partitions for AD LDS instances?

Answer:

We can create application partitions for AD LDS instances in three ways:

a) By initiating AD LDS related application installation that will be attached to an AD LDS instance

b) By creating a new instance during the installation of AD LDS instance

c) By manually creating application partition by using LDP.exe command line utility

This page is intentionally left blank

Active Directory Users Groups and Computers

67: A user logs on to a Domain using User1@Datacorp.com credentials. What is the other credential method of logging on to a Domain?

Answer:

A user can also logon as DATACORP\User1 where DATACORP is the NetBIOS name of the domain followed by a backslash (\) and username which is User1.

68: You are an Administrator in a company. You have three sites, Sydney, Dallas and New Delhi. CEO of the organization has decided to dissolve Dallas branch. When you attempt to remove all OUs created for Dallas site it responds as: The object is protected from accidental deletion. What will you do to delete this Organizational Unit (OU)?

Answer:

In Active Directory Users and Computers snap-in click View menu and select Advanced Features. Then right-click on the target OU and click Properties. Go to Object tab and uncheck Protect object from accidental deletion check box. Save changes and finally delete the Organizational Unit.

69: You are the administrator of a company named DATACORP.COM. You hired a tech support engineer so that you can delegate some administrative task of adding users, creating users and resetting user passwords to him. Which tool or feature will you use to do so?

Answer:

Windows Server 2008 R2 has a built-in feature named

Delegation of Control that can be used to solve the purpose. With the help of Delegation of Controls even non-admin users can be granted some admin privileges (specified by admins only) without adding them to Administrators group.

70: What is an Organizational Unit (OU)?

Answer:

Organizational Unit is a container that administrators can create on the domain controllers which can contain multiple domain objects. Difference between a normal container e.g. Users and an OU is that administrators can link Group Policy Objects (GPOs) to the OUs but not to standard containers.

71: You are the administrator of a company named DATACORP.COM. When you initiated Active Directory Users and Computers snap-in, you found that one of the users' icons in Users container has a small down arrow. What does it mean?

Answer:

This means that the user account is disabled.

72: How many scopes does a domain group have?

Answer:

There are three main scopes that can be used while creating a domain group, namely

a) **Domain Local Group:** Can contain User Accounts, Global and Universal groups from any domain but can contain Domain Local groups from the same domain.

b) **Global Group:** Can contain User Accounts and Global groups of same domain.

c) **Universal Group:** Can contain User Accounts, Global and Universal groups from any domain in the forest.

73: What is secondary logon?

Answer:

Secondary logon is a service that allows users to provide alternate credentials (mostly administrative) without logging off from the current user account. When users right click on any application in the context menu, Run as Administrator option is displayed. If the logged on user account belongs to non-administrator group, Windows displays a dialog box where users can provide administrative credentials.

74: What is UPN suffix?

Answer:

User Principal Name or UPN Suffix is an alternate suffix that can be added to a domain user name. If there are multiple domains and domain trees in an active directory forest, a user account may have a lengthy UPN suffix, for example username@rootdomain.childdomain.com. With the help of alternate UPN suffix it can be username@alternateupnsuffix.com. This makes it simpler for users to type their credentials.

75: What is the difference between local users and domain users?

Answer:

In any computer when user accounts are stored and authenticated from the local Security Accounts Manager or SAM file they are known as local user accounts. On the other hand when the account credentials are sent to the domain controllers for authentication, such type of user accounts are known as domain user accounts.

76: Why do you create a shadow group?
Answer:

We cannot link a Password Security Object (PSO) to an Organizational Unit (OU) directly. Instead we create a security group called as Shadow Group that contains all associated user accounts from an OU to which we want to apply PSOs. Shadow Groups must be created manually.

77: By default, members of which group can create Password Setting Objects (PSOs)?
Answer:

Members of Domain Admins group can create and/or modify PSOs.

78: What type of Active Directory objects a Universal Group can contain?
Answer:

Universal group in an active directory infrastructure can contain universal groups that exist in any other domain of the forest, global groups that may reside in any domain of the forest and user accounts that may reside in any domain of the forest.

79: In which environment should you use Distribution groups?

Answer:

Distribution groups are mostly used in an Exchange Server oriented environment.

DHCP

80: What is the purpose of creating reservations in DHCP?

Answer:

In complex network scenarios where DHCP servers are used to assign dynamic IP addresses to the client computers, sometimes administrators might want DHCP servers to assign a particular IP address to a particular computer every time it requests for the address. In such situations administrators must create DHCP reservations in which they map the MAC address of a client computer with the IP address available in the DHCP server. Once this is done every time the client computer starts and requests for an IP address from the DHCP server, DHCP server assigns the predefined IP address from its pool to the requesting client computer.

81: When does a client obtain an IP address of 169.254.0.0/16 range?

Answer:

When a client computer is configured to obtain IP address from the DHCP server and because of any reason if DHCP server is not available, the operating system automatically assigns an IP address to itself. This feature is known as Automatic Private IP Addressing or APIPA and the IP address that is self-signed falls in the range of 169.254.0.0 with default subnet mask of 255.255.0.0.

82: What is a Super Scope?

Answer:

Super Scope in a DHCP server can be considered as a container that can contain multiple DHCP scopes of different subnets. Scopes that a DHCP super scope contains are known as member scopes.

83: When does a DHCP client request DHCP server for IP address renewal?

Answer:

When an IP address is assigned to a computer via DHCP server it requests for the renewal of the IP address after the 50% of its lease duration is lapsed. If the DHCP server is not available it waits for some more time and again requests for renewal. If DHCP server is still not available, the DHCP client sends a broadcast DHCP Discover packet to hunt for new IP address from other DHCP servers available in the network.

84: What is the default lease duration for which an IP address is assigned to a client computer by the DHCP server?

Answer:

When a client computer requests an IP address from the DHCP server, default lease duration for which the IP address is assigned to the client computer is eight days. This default duration can be increased or decreased as per the network infrastructure and employees that work in the organization.

85: Describe the process of DORA.

Answer:

D: DHCP Discover: A broadcast message sent by DHCP clients to search for DHCP server on the network

O: DHCP Offer: A unicast message sent by DHCP server to the requesting client offering available IP address from its address pool

R: DHCP Request: A unicast message sent to DHCP server from the client requesting for offered IP address

A: DHCP Acknowledgement: A unicast message sent from DHCP server to DHCP client confirming the allocation of offered IP address

86: What is the function of DHCP relay agent?
Answer:

In a network environment where there are multiple subnets involved and there is only one DHCP server that is located in one subnet, DHCP relay agents are configured in all other subnets which receive DHCP discover requests from the DHCP clients and forward them to the DHCP server as a unicast message.

87: What do you understand by exclusions in DHCP?
Answer:

In a DHCP oriented network infrastructure many times administrators might not want a particular IP address from DHCP address pool to be assigned to any client computer. In such cases administrators exclude those IP addresses from getting automatically assigned and this process is known as exclusions in DHCP.

88: When you configure ICS what IP address is assigned to

the internal network adapter?

Answer:

When ICS or Internet Connection Sharing is enabled the NIC that is shared is automatically converted to a mini DHCP server and it starts assigning IP addresses from Class C private IP address range which is 192.168.0.0/24.

89: What is the difference between DHCP and DHCPv6?

Answer:

Major difference between DHCP and DHCPv6 is that DHCP dynamically assigns IPv4 addresses to the client computers whereas DHCPv6 assigns IPv6 addresses to the clients. DHCP supports the process called DORA whereas in DHCPv6 DORA is replaced by a SOLICIT message. DHCPv6 clients can request multiple IPv6 addresses whereas IPv4 clients can request only one IPv4 IP address.

This page is intentionally left blank

IP Addressing

90: What is the loopback address in IPv6?

Answer:

Loopback address from IPv6 is ::1.

91: How many bits are there in an IPv6 address?

Answer:

IPv6 contains 128 bits.

92: What are Global addresses in IPv6?

Answer:

Public addresses in IPv4 are replaced by global addresses in IPv6 which are globally reachable on the IPv6 based internet.

93: What is Link Local Multicast Name Resolution (LLMNR) method?

Answer:

Subnets that have no DNS infrastructure use LLMNR for name resolution. It can only be configured on the computers running Windows Vista, Windows 7, Windows Server 2008 and Windows Server 2008 R2. IPv6 and Network Discovery must be enabled on the computers.

94: Which protocol replaces the Address Resolution Protocol (ARP) in IPv6?

Answer:

Network Discovery (ND) protocol replaces Address Resolution Protocol (ARP) in IPv6.

95: Which protocol connects IPv6 hosts and routers over IPv4 networks?

Answer:

Intra-site Automatic Tunnel Addressing Protocol (ISATAP) is used to connect IPv6 hosts and routers over IPv4 networks.

96: What are the different types of IPv6 transition strategies?

Answer:

There are three types of transition strategies from IPv4 to IPv6:-

a) **Intra-site Automatic Tunnel Addressing Protocol (ISATAP):** Allows computers with IPv6 address to communicate with computers configured with IPv4 addresses.

b) **6to4:** Is a tunneling protocol that helps computers having IPv6 addresses communicate with external networks that use IPv4 addressing scheme.

c) **Teredo Tunneling Protocol:** Is a tunneling protocol used to allow Network Address Translation (NAT) between computers with IPv6 and IPv4 addresses.

This page is intentionally left blank

Network and Application
Infrastructure

97: What is a RADIUS Server?

Answer:

Remote Authentication Dial In User Service or RADIUS server is dedicated computer that is responsible for centralized Authentication, Authorization and Accounting (AAA). RADIUS is used in the setups where there are several computers scattered around the globe and require authentication from the active directory database.

98: Which protocol is used for smart card authentication?

Answer:

Extensible Authentication Protocol-Transport Layer Security or EAP-TLS is the protocol that supports Smart Card authentication.

99: What is Distributed File System (DFS)?

Answer:

Distributed File System or DFS helps administrators to efficiently manage shared resources stored on file servers. With help of DFS administrators can centralize the accessibility of shared objects that can otherwise be scattered on multiple computers in the network. When Distributed File System or DFS is configured all scattered objects (files and folders) can be stored under a domain wide DFS namespace that can be accessed by any domain user.

100: Name the types of VPN tunneling protocol.

Answer:

There are three VPN tunneling protocols that are mostly used nowadays, namely PPTP - Point-to-Point Tunneling Protocol, L2TP - Layer 2 Tunneling Protocol and SSTP - Secure Socket Tunneling Protocol.

101: What are the prerequisites for deploying Windows Deployment Services (WDS)?

Answer:

Windows Deployment Services or WDS is used to deploy operating systems on remote computers via network. In order to install and use Windows Deployment Services in a network the network must have at least one domain controller, a DHCP server and DNS server available and well-connected.

102: What is Hyper-V or Hypervisor?

Answer:

Hypervisor is a role in Windows Server 2008 R2 operating system which when installed allows administrators to configure several virtual machines on a single computer. This helps organizations establish cost-effective network infrastructure by using a single physical computer that has multiple virtual machines. In all, Hyper-V eliminates the requirement of purchasing multiple physical computers hence remarkably saving the cost of the hardware.

103: Which TCP port is used to initiate RDP connections to terminal servers?

Answer:

TCP 339 is used for RDP connections for both Remote Desktop and Remote Assistance.

104: What do you understand by the term DFS namespace?

Answer:

DFS namespace is a domain-wide globally accepted name that is used by the users when they need access to shared objects. DFS centralizes all shared objects and DFS Namespace is used to identify the location from where the shared objects can be accessed. An example for a DFS Namespace may be AllSharedFolders. This namespace can be accessed by using UNC path and the name of the domain, e.g. \\mydomain\AllSharedFolders.

105: Why Windows Server Update Services (WSUS) server is used?

Answer:

Windows Server Update Services (WSUS) Server is used to manage updates from the Microsoft Website for all clients in a network. WSUS server downloads the updates and distributes them to the client computers according to their needs and roles they play in the network. WSUS server prevents excessive consumption of internet bandwidth by downloading updates on behalf of client computers.

106: What do you understand by printer pooling?

Answer:

Printer pooling allows load balancing to the printers when an organization has large number of employees and extensive printing is required. When printer pooling is enabled print requests are equally distributed among all printers that are members of a printer pool. In order to create a printer pool all participating printers must be of the same vendor and identical model.

107: How many maximum concurrent Remote Desktop sessions can be initiated on a computer running Windows Server 2008 R2?

Answer:

By default maximum two Remote Desktop sessions can be created on Windows Server 2008 R2 computer. Users must have administrative privileges on the computer to which Remote Desktop sessions are to be established.

108: What is the changed name of Terminal Services in Windows Server 2008 R2?

Answer:

Terminal Services is replaced by RemoteApp and Desktop (RAD) connections feature, which is the combination of Remote Desktop Services (RDS) and Virtual Desktop Infrastructure (VDI) using which virtual machines can also be accessed from remote computers.

109: In a RADIUS oriented environment, who acts as a radius client?

Answer:

Routing and Remote Access Server (RRAS).

110: What are the major Distributed File System (DFS) elements?

Answer:

Major Distributed File System (DFS) elements are:

a) **Namespace:** A globally recognized name to locate DFS root

b) **Namespace Server:** A dedicated file server that holds DFS root

c) **Namespace Root:** Main DFS root that contains several shared objects under common roof which might be otherwise scattered in the absence of DFS

d) **Folder:** A link of the folder that can be accessed while accessing DFS

e) **Folder Targets:** Actual folders to which DFS folders point. Folder Targets contain files and other objects. When DFS Folders are created, they must point to the Folder Targets to make objects available to the users

111: Which port is used by Remote Desktop Gateway to communicate with clients over SSL?

Answer:

Port number 443 is used by Remote Desktop Gateway to communicate with clients over SSL.

112: What is the benefit of FTPS over FTP?

Answer:

Secure File Transfer Protocol or FTPS uses secure channel while transferring files from source to destination whereas File Transfer Protocol or FTP transfers data in an unencrypted form which can be read by any unauthorized user if captured.

113: Which command is used to initiate IIS 7.5 Manager?
Answer:
To start IIS 7.5 Manager, start inetmgr command is used.

114: Which streaming protocol is used by Windows media services?
Answer:
Real-Time Streaming protocol (RTSP) is used by Windows media services.

115: What are the system requirements for deploying Hyper-V in Windows Server 2008 R2?
Answer:
a) Host Operating System: Windows Server 2008 or 2008 R2 Enterprise, Standard or Datacenter (64- bit editions only)
b) An x86-64 bit platform based processor, with Virtualization Technology (VT) support
c) Minimum 2 GB memory or more for each Guest OS is recommended

116: How many logical cores does a single instance and single Virtual Machine instance of Windows Server 2008 R2

support?

Answer:

A single instance of Windows Sever 2008 R2 supports up to 256 logical processors and single instance of Virtual Machine can support up to 32 logical cores.

Security

117: You are the Administrator of a company. For security reason management decided that a particular user must not logon after 4.00 p.m. What appropriate action will you take?

Answer:

In Active Directory Users and Computers snap-in right-click the target user and click Properties. On Account tab click Logon Hours and drag your mouse to restrict time.

118: You have created a shared folder in a file server and you want that Marketing group can access the shared folder but Accounts group cannot. What will you do?

Answer:

NTFS permissions must be set to Allow for Marketing group. Accounts group must not be added in the Access Control List (ACL) which would automatically set Implicit Deny permissions for the group.

119: Your Company undertakes a new project and you want to give access to your domain partner on your file server to a specific folder. What type of group will you create so that they can access that folder?

Answer:

Create a Domain Local Security Group on your Domain Controller and nest Universal Security Group of your domain partner into it. Then set 'Allow' NTFS permission to this Domain Local Security Group by adding its name in the ACL of the shared folder.

Note: Domain Local security groups can contain any member or group from any trusted domain.

120: What is the difference between authentication and authorization?

Answer:

Authentication is the process through which users' identification is verified whereas authorization means what privileges users get after they have been successfully authenticated.

121: Describe the benefits provided by the SSL (Secure Sockets Layer).

Answer:

With the help of Secure Socket Layer communication that takes place between the client machine and server remains encrypted.

122: What do you understand by Network Level Authentication?

Answer:

Network Level Authentication or NLA is a technology that was introduced in Microsoft Windows Vista and is carried forward to the latest operating systems. Network Level Authentication requires users to provide their credentials for authentication to the remote computers before they actually connect to them while using Remote Desktop Connection that uses Remote Desktop Protocol or RDP.

123: What do you understand by the term Kerberos authentication?

Answer:

Kerberos authentication is a process in which when users provide their credentials to logon to the domain, Kerberos protocol transfers the credentials to the domain controllers. Once the credentials are authenticated by the DC, tickets are generated and are sent to the users. Kerberos protocol participates in this process as well.

124: Why do we need DRA?

Answer:

Data recovery agent or DRA is a user account that has privileges of decrypting the encrypted files. In any network infrastructure it is recommended that users must encrypt their files in order to avoid unauthorized access. If because of any reason users fail to decrypt the files or user accounts are deleted, Data Recovery Agents can decrypt files using recovery keys.

125: What is Transport Layer Security (TLS)?

Answer:

Transport Layer Security is the protocol that encrypts the segments of network connections at transport layer. It is a cryptography protocol used to provide communication security over the internet by keeping the integrity of the messages intact.

126: What is Access Control List (ACL)?

Answer:

Access Control List is a set of rules for computers or users using which administrators can allow or deny their access to the resources.

127: What is Domain Isolation Policy?

Answer:

Domain Isolation Policy is a security rule created in Windows Firewall and Advance Security through which internal network or domain members can be isolated from the external or public domains. This configuration is done to prevent hackers from identifying and entering internal networks.

128: What is BitLocker Drive Encryption?

Answer:

BitLocker Drive Encryption is an encryption feature which is used to protect data by encrypting entire Volumes or Disks using a key pair. It uses AES encryption algorithm. BitLocker was first introduced in Windows Vista and was carried forward and made more efficient in Windows 7, Windows Server 2008 and Windows Server 2008 R2 operating systems.

This page is intentionally left blank

Name Resolution in Windows Server 2008 R2

129: You have established a domain/client network infrastructure using Windows Server 2008 R2 and have named the domain as DATACORP.COM. What will be the NetBIOS name of the domain?

Answer:

NetBIOS name for DATACORP.COM domain will be DATACORP.

130: You are an Administrator of DATACORP.COM. When you try to add a client computer to DATACORP.COM domain it gives an error saying: An Active Directory Domain Controller for the domain DATACORP.COM could not be contacted. How will you resolve this problem?

Answer:

In most cases this happens because of inappropriate DNS addresses defined in client computers. The administrator must correct the Preferred DNS Server address specified at the client computer. If DNS IP address is not an issue, other reasons might be disconnected network cable, DNS failure, etc.

131: In IP v4 DNS representation of host records is A. What is the representation of host records in IP v6?

Answer:

DNS representation of Host records that use IP v6 is AAAA.

132: What are Root Hints?

Answer:

Root Hints in DNS server is list of third-party DNS servers that are located on the internet. When a local DNS server or the DNS server of an ISP fails to resolve the query, the query is forwarded to Root Hints servers. There are around 13 Root Hint DNS servers.

133: Why do we need to configure conditional forwarders?

Answer:

When a query is sent to local DNS server and it fails to resolve, the query is then forwarded to Root Hints servers. If administrators want to forward some queries that look for another domain configured in the forest (which is not an external or public domain), administrators must configure conditional forwarding so that the queries are sent to the DNS servers of the requested domains only instead of getting forwarded to the external DNS servers.

134: You are the administrator of a company named DATACORP.COM that has two sites, Dallas and Sydney. Both sites have DNS Servers. Sites are connected via 256 Kbps WAN link. To save your bandwidth and for better query resolution, you created a stub zone for Sydney site in Dallas site but when you attempt to reload the zone or transfer from master it gives an error- Unable to transfer from master. What could be the real cause?

Answer:

Zone transfers must be enabled in Zone Transfer tab of the DNS server in Dallas.

135: Why do you need to configure scavenging and aging on a DNS server?

Answer:

Aging and Scavenging are configured to specify maximum age of DNS records and to automatically remove them when they are expired.

136: When do we need to configure Forwarders?

Answer:

When there are multiple DNS servers in a network, by default they forward queries to Root Hints if they fail to resolve them on their own. This configuration might be quite bandwidth consuming. To solve this problem administrators normally configure a dedicated multi-homed machine as DNS forwarder and configure all other DNS servers to forward unsolved queries to the dedicated DNS forwarder. Forwarders on their parts forward the queries to external DNS servers for name resolutions.

137: What do you understand by DNS recursion?

Answer:

When a DNS client requests for an IP address for any host name, the query is sent to the local DNS server. Local DNS server, on its part, then first checks its local cache and if it fails to resolve the query it forwards the request to the external DNS server in order to resolve the query on behalf of client computer. This process is known as DNS recursion.

138: What types of records does a stub zone contain?

Answer:

Stub zone contains only Start of Authority (SOA) and Name Servers (NS) records that are authoritative for their respective domains.

139: In which scenario we can use Caching Only DNS Server?

Answer:

Caching Only DNS Server is the default configuration of a DNS server that is automatically configured when DNS server is installed. This configuration can be left intact and is best suited for small-scale organizations where client computers do not exceed 20 or 25 in number.

140: Which resource records are used to resolve queries for Exchange Server?

Answer:

Mail-Exchanger (MX) records are used to resolve Exchange Server queries.

141: Describe the process of how Secondary DNS server receives DNS records from Master DNS server.

Answer:

In order to transfer DNS records from Master DNS server to the Secondary DNS server, zone transfers must be enabled in Zone Transfers tab of the Master DNS server. Once this is done appropriate radio button must be selected by the administrators to allow Secondary DNS server to request and receive DNS records from the Master DNS server.

142: What is the use of stub zone?

Answer:

Stub zone in DNS server is used when master DNS server contains large number of DNS records and the administrators do not want to configure secondary DNS servers because of bandwidth consuming replication process. Stub zones contain only the Start of Authority (SOA) records and the Name Servers (NS) records of the domains for which they are authoritative. This configuration remarkably reduces Internet bandwidth consumption as it completely eliminates the requirement of DNS zone replications.

143: What is Active Directory integrated zone?

Answer:

When a DNS server is installed in peer-to-peer networks DNS database is stored in a file that has .dns extension. However when the network infrastructure is domain/client based the default configuration of DNS server is that it stores its database within the active directory database, that is, NTDS.dit file and this is known as Active Directory integrated zone. This is the default configuration and is most recommended as it provides optimum security and eliminates the initialization of manual DNS replication process.

144: What do you understand by DNS suffix?

Answer:

DNS suffix is the name of the domain that is added to the hostname and helps a host computer to become easily identifiable in the entire domain. When a computer is added to a domain, DNS suffix is automatically added to the hostname and is separated by a dot (.) which technically is known as a period. An example for this can be computer1.microsoft.com.

145: What do you understand by the Glue Record?

Answer:

Glue Records are the IP addresses that point to the Name Servers in any DNS oriented network infrastructure.

146: What are Pointer (PTR) records?

Answer:

PTR records resolve host names on the basis of their IP addresses. Pointer (PTR) records can only be created when administrators create Reverse Lookup Zones. Moreover, NSLOOKUP command only works successfully if Reverse Lookup Zone is created.

147: What is NetBIOS name resolution?

Answer:

NetBIOS name resolution is when the server resolves a single-label name. DNS server only resolves Fully Qualified Domain Names or FQDNs. To resolve NetBIOS names either WINS servers were used in earlier days or administrators used to add primary DNS suffixes to the host names manually if they had DNS servers present in the networks. In Windows Server 2008 a new feature named GlobalNames Zone (GNZ) is introduced which eliminates the requirement of WINS server and still resolves single-label names.

148: What is GlobalNames Zone?

Answer:

GlobalNames Zone is a new feature introduced in Microsoft Windows Server 2008 which allows single-label (NetBIOS) name resolution. This feature is introduced to replace WINS, hence completely eliminating its requirement.

149: Name the scopes available for DNS Zone replication in Active Directory infrastructure.

Answer:

There are four scopes where DNS Zones can be replicated in Active Directory infrastructure:

a) To all DNS servers in the Active Directory Forest
b) To all DNS servers in the Active Directory Domain
c) To all domain controllers in an Active Directory Domain
d) To all domain controllers specified in the scope of the following application directory partition (Custom list required)

150: What are Name Servers?

Answer:

Name Server is a dedicated computer that is responsible to resolve DNS queries initiated by client computers. Sometimes

DNS server is also referred as Name Server.

151: What is the use of LMhosts file?

Answer:

Lmhost file is used to resolve NetBIOS names to their respective IP addresses. IP addresses must be manually specified in the Lmhost file.

152: Why should you configure alternate DNS server address?

Answer:

In medium or large-scale industries administrators mostly deploy multiple DNS servers so that if one server fails entire network does not get affected because of lack of name resolution system. In such scenarios administrators specify preferred and alternate DNS server addresses to the client computers so that if because of any reason preferred DNS server fails to resolve the query, the query can be sent to the alternate DNS server for name resolution.

153: What are the DNS zone transfer options available in the Zone Transfers tab in Windows Server 2008 R2?

Answer:

There are three options available in the Zone Transfers tab-

a) To any server

b) Only to servers listed on the Name Server Tab

c) Only to the following servers (Custom list of DNS server must be specified).

154: What is the newly added feature in Windows Server 2008 R2 which allows client computers to verify the authenticity of the DNS record?

Answer:

DNSSEC is the feature which checks the integrity of DNS query responses through public key technologies.

155: What is the use of cache.dns file and where it is found?

Answer:

Cache.dns file stores DNS cache which is used by DNS server to resolve names over internet. It contains the list of available internet root servers. It can be located in %systemroot%\system32\DNS directory.

156: What is BIND in DNS?

Answer:

Berkley Internet Name Domain (BIND) is a means of transferring zone data that is used by UNIX based operating systems because they do not use fast transfer format. When Windows based computers perform zone transfer to UNIX based operating systems BIND is used. This option is enabled by-default.

157: What is the difference between Forward Lookup and Reverse Lookup Zone?

Answer:

Forward lookup zone is configured to resolve Fully Qualified Domain Names to IP addresses whereas Reverse lookup zone is configured to resolve IP addresses to Fully Qualified Domain Names.

158: In which condition can we store a DNS zone in Active Directory?

Answer:

In any active directory oriented network infrastructure when an active directory domain controller also plays a role of DNS server, by default DNS database is stored in Active Directory database. This default DNS configuration is known as DNS integrated zone.

This page is intentionally left blank

Disk Management and
Storage

159: What is the difference between basic disk and dynamic disk?

Answer:

One of the major differences between basic disks and dynamic disks is that dynamic disks can be used to implement Redundant Array of Inexpensive Disks (RAIDs) and are mostly used in production environments whereas normal disk types are mostly used in home environments. When an operating system is installed on a hard disk drive by default it is set as a basic disk. Administrators must manually convert basic disks to dynamic disks.

160: What is the difference between Network Attached Storage (NAS) and Direct Attached Storage (DAS)?

Answer:

Network Attached Storage devices are those that are not directly connected to the computers and are centrally located and connected to the network. In such cases data is backed up and stored on these devices as per the schedule which remarkably reduces administrators' overhead that they would otherwise have to face if the devices were connected locally. These devices are helpful when there are multiple file servers and domain controllers in the network.

Direct Attached Storage devices are the ones that are directly connected to the computers and backups are stored on them. These devices are useful when there is only one or maximum two file servers or domain controllers in a network.

161: What do you understand by Network Load Balancing Cluster?

Answer:

Network Load Balancing or NLB is a cluster configuration that allows administrators to equally balance the load of traffic among all the members in a cluster. With the help of NLB, queries are distributed among the servers of a cluster on round robin basis. For example if there are three servers in a cluster namely A, B and C first query will be sent to server A, second to server B and third to server C. When the cluster receives fourth query it will be sent to server A and so on.

162: What is SMB?

Answer:

Server Message Block or SMB is a protocol that is used to provide access to the shared resources located at the file servers. Sometimes SMB is also known as Common Internet File System or CIFS. SMB is an application layer protocol.

163: Why offline files are important?

Answer:

Offline files are important if an organization has multiple users who work on part-time basis and their job includes working from homes as well. In such cases administrators configure offline files so that these mobile users can save cached copies of the files on their local machines on which they can work even when they are not connected to the office network.

164: What are RAID volumes?

Answer:

RAID volumes are the hard disk drives that are logically bundled together to work as a single entity so as to provide fault tolerance and additional storage capacity. In order to implement RAIDs, hard disks must be converted to dynamic disk types.

165: What is Network File System (NFS)?

Answer:

Network File System (NFS) is a protocol used to access shared resources efficiently. When any object or resource is accessed from a remote location, because of NFS the operating system looks at the remote entities as local objects or resources stored on a local storage media.

166: What is Cluster Shared Volumes (CSV)?

Answer:

Cluster Shared Volumes is a feature which is introduced in Windows Server 2008 R2 and is used in conjunction with Hyper-V. With the help of this feature administrators can access multiple virtual hard disk files from all cluster nodes simultaneously.

167: Why do we need to configure Disk quota?

Answer:

In complex production environments many times administrators configure roaming user profiles and they configure user files to be saved on a centrally located file server. In order to restrict and limit users from occupying large disk spaces, administrators mostly configure Disk Quotas so that users can only utilize the hard disk spaces that administrators manually assign to them.

168: What is the difference between Hard Quota and Soft Quota?

Answer:

When administrators assign disk quotas they can choose any one of the two available options. They can either restrict users from saving files on the quota enabled volumes if they exceed their quota limits or they can allow users to continue saving their files even if their quota limits exceed, but with warning messages. When administrators restrict users from saving files on quota enabled volume this is known as Hard Quota and when users are allowed to save files even if the quota limit expires this is known as Soft Quota.

169: What is a Witness Disk?

Answer:

Witness Disks are the shared volumes that contain copies of cluster configuration databases. In Windows Server 2003, Witness Disks were known as Quorum Disks. These disks are connected as a central storage media for the servers that participate as members of the cluster.

170: Which editions of Windows Sever 2008 R2 support

failover clustering?

Answer:

Only Enterprise and Datacenter editions of Windows Server 2008 R2 support failover clustering.

Backup and Restore

171: What is Volume Shadow Copy?

Answer:

Volume Shadow Copy is a feature integrated in Microsoft Windows operating systems that allows administrators to capture snapshots of the data which can be restored in case actual data is lost. Administrators must manually enable Volume Shadow Copy feature for each volume individually.

172: What is Bare Metal restore?

Answer:

Bare Metal Restore is a technique through which administrators can restore all backed up data in a fresh machine that has no Operating System or software installed.

173 What is the command line tool used to performing an Active Directory authoritative restore?

Answer:

Ntdsutil command is used to perform authoritative restore.

174: How can you perform a Non-Authoritative Restore?

Answer:

Non-Authoritative Restore can be performed by navigating Windows Server backup console or by typing Wbadmin.exe on command line.

175: What is the main benefit of restoring Active Directory using Installation from Media (IFM) process?

Answer:

With the help of Installation from Media or IFM process, when an Active Directory is restored on a Windows Server 2008 R2 computer from a backup, it remarkably reduces administrator's overhead which they would otherwise have to face if they had to install Active Directory Domain Services on a bare metal machine and wait for replication to get all configuration and settings.

This page is intentionally left blank

Scripting

176: As an administrator of DATACORP.COM you need to create 200 domain user accounts. How will you complete the task with least administrative overhead?

Answer:

As an administrator I shall create PowerShell or VBScripts to automate user creation task. In order to accomplish this, I will create a .ps1 file that will contain command to create user accounts. Once the file is created I will call it in PowerShell interface by using ".\".

177: Which command is used to manage SYSVOL replication when Forest Functional Level is Windows Server 2008 R2?

Answer:

DFSRadmin.exe command is used to manage SYSVOL replication in Windows Server 2008 R2 when Forest Functional Level is raised to Windows Server 2008 R2. DFSR is also used during Active Directory replication. In legacy versions of Windows Network Operating Systems, File Replication Services (FRS) was used.

178: Which command-line utility is used to perform initial configuration of WDS (Windows Deployment Services) Server in Windows Server 2008 R2?

Answer:

Wdsutil is the command-line utility through which we can configure WDS (Windows Deployment Services) Server.

179: Which command is used to enable Active Directory

Recycle Bin feature in Windows Server 2008 R2?

Answer:

We can type the following command in Windows Powershell module:

Enable-ADOptionalFeature -Identity <ADOptionalFeature> - Scope <ADOptionalFeatureScope> -Target <ADEntity>.

For example if we want to enable Active Directory Recycle bin for mydomain.com domain, we should type:

Enable-ADOptionalFeature –Identity 'CN=Recycle Bin Feature,CN=Optional Features,CN=Directory Service,CN=Windows NT,CN=Services,CN=Configuration,DC=mydomain,DC=com'- Scope ForestOrConfigurationSet –Target 'mydomain.com'

180: What does OOBE command do?

Answer:

When Windows Server 2008 R2 is installed, the very first window that appears on the screen is Initial Configuration Tasks. After administrators have configured their servers with appropriate settings they can disable the initialization of this window at every startup. However if because of any reason they still want to access this window they can type in Out-Of-Box Experience (OOBE) command in the search box or Run command box to initiate it.

181: Which command line tool is used to troubleshoot DNS server?

Answer:

Nslookup command is used to troubleshoot DNS server from command line.

182: Through which command we can convert a Security Policy into a Group Policy Object (GPO)?

Answer:

Scwcmd.exe transform command converts a Security Policy into a GPO.

183: Which command is used to update Group Policy settings on a client computer?

Answer:

Gpupdate.exe or gpupdate /force command can be executed in the elevated command prompt on the client computer.

184: Which command is used to manage DNS server from command line?

Answer:

Dnscmd command can be used to manage DNS server from command line utility.

185: Which command is used to renew an IP address assigned by DHCP server?

Answer:

In order to renew dynamic IP address assigned by DHCP server ipconfig /renew command must be executed from the elevated command prompt.

186: Which command you must use to deploy Read Only Domain Controller (RODC)?

Answer:

Although deployment of Read Only Domain Controller (RODC) can be made simpler through GUI, adprep /rodcprep command can be used to create RODC through command line interface.

187: Why do we initiate ipconfig /flushdns command?

Answer:

It clears DNS cache from the client computers.

188: What command is used to add client computers to a specific DHCP User Class?

Answer:

IPCONFIG /SetClassID is the command that administrators must use on all client computers to add them to a specific DHCP User Class.

189: Which command line utility is used to administer Windows SharePoint Services?

Answer:

Stsadm.exe is the command line utility that is used to administer Windows SharePoint Services (WSS).

190: What is Windows PowerShell?

Answer:

Windows PowerShell was introduced with the release of

Microsoft Windows Server 2008 RTM and is now carried forward to Microsoft Windows Server 2008 R2 operating system. Windows PowerShell provides CLI or Command Line Interface in which users and administrators can run commands. Moreover Windows PowerShell is a scripting platform which administrators can use to create and execute scripts to automate administrative tasks.

Group Policy Objects

191: What are Starter GPOs?

Answer:

A Starter GPO contains Administrative templates. Starter GPOs can be configured with the settings which administrators want to pre-configure while creating Group Policy Objects (GPOs). When administrators create GPOs they must configure every created GPO right from the scratch and some GPOs must have identical settings to be configured. Without Starter GPOs this would have been a tedious task. Starter GPOs allow administrators to configure identical settings just once and then the Starter GPOs can be called while creating GPOs.

192: Being an Administrator of DATACORP.COM you have configured a GPO named DesktopLock that has following settings:

a) **Remove Add or Remove Programs**

b) **Restrict Access to Control Panel**

c) **Prevent changing desktop wallpaper**

You want to link it to an OU named DatacorpUsers which also contains a child OU named Executives. What will you do to prevent Executives OU from inheriting settings from DesktopLock GPO?

Answer:

A Parent Organizational Unit (OU) can contain multiple Child OUs. By default, when a GPO is linked to a parent OU its child OUs automatically inherit the settings. To prevent the settings from being inherited by child OUs, inheritance on child OUs must be blocked by the administrators manually.

193: You are an administrator at DATACORP.COM. For security reasons, you want that users cannot plug any USB or removable devices to the computers. What appropriate action you should take to do so?

Answer:

A separate GPO in which removable and plug and play devices are restricted must be created and linked to the domain using Group Policy Management Console (GPMC). Furthermore, this GPO must be enforced by right clicking on the GPO and clicking Enforced option so that even if some OUs have been configured to block inheritance, this group policy setting still becomes applicable on them.

194: In which condition you are required to configure Loopback Policy Processing?

Answer:

When an Organizational Unit (OU) is linked to the Group Policy Object (GPO) that has been configured with both User Configuration and Computer Configuration and administrators want that if a particular computer is shared in public places, such as reception area, only Computer Configuration takes precedence irrespective of the user account that logs on to the computer. In such cases Loopback Policy Processing is used which enforces Computer Configuration of the GPO to be applied on the publicly shared computer.

195: You want to install Microsoft Word 2007 on all your client computers in the network. How would you accomplish

the task with least administrative overhead?

Answer:

Installing MS Office package on every client computer individually would be a tedious task. In such case administrators must use Group Policies to deploy the package domain wide. They can choose either Published or Assigned mode to accomplish the task.

196: What are fine grained policies in Windows Server 2008 R2?

Answer:

Fine Grained Policies help administrators to specify different sets of policies for different users or groups. In earlier versions of Windows, operating systems only allowed administrators to assign group policies on Site, Domain or Organizational Unit level. With the release of Windows Server 2008 RTM/R2, feature of fine grained policies is introduced which allows administrators to assign policies on per-user or per-group basis.

197: Name the two built-in GPOs that are by default created when AD DS is installed.

Answer:

The two built-in GPOs are Default Domain Policy and Default Domain Controller Policy.

198: What is the difference between Default Domain Policy and Default Domain Controller Policy?

Answer:

Default Domain Policy is applied throughout the domain and is effective on every object and organizational unit that a domain contains. On the other hand, Default Domain Controller Policy is linked only to Domain Controllers organizational unit and is applicable to all domain controllers that reside in that OU.

199: What are the two ways of deploying software through group policies?

Answer:

Two ways to deploy software applications through group policies are:

a) **Assigned (Computer Configuration and User Configuration):** In this type of deployment applications automatically get installed as soon as computer starts or user logs on.

b) **Published (User Configuration):** In this deployment type users must manually install available applications by going to Add or Remove Programs in Control Panel of client computers.

200: What is the difference between assigning an application and publishing an application in Group Policy?

Answer:

While deploying software applications through group policies, when the deployment type is set as assigned, applications automatically get installed as soon as the computers start or the users log on. On the other hand when the deployment type is set as published, users must go to Control Panel and must manually install the applications before they can use them.

HR Questions

Review these typical interview questions and think about how you would answer them. Read the answers listed; you will find best possible answers along with strategies and suggestions.

1: How would you handle a negative coworker?

Answer:

Everyone has to deal with negative coworkers – and the single best way to do so is to remain positive. You may try to build a relationship with the coworker or relate to them in some way, but even if your efforts are met with a cold shoulder, you must retain your positive attitude. Above all, stress that you would never allow a coworker's negativity to impact your own work or productivity.

2: What would you do if you witnessed a coworker surfing the web, reading a book, etc, wasting company time?

Answer:

The interviewer will want to see that you realize how detrimental it is for employees to waste company time, and that it is not something you take lightly. Explain the way you would adhere to company policy, whether that includes talking to the coworker yourself, reporting the behavior straight to a supervisor, or talking to someone in HR.

3: How do you handle competition among yourself and other employees?

Answer:

Healthy competition can be a great thing, and it is best to stay focused on the positive aspects of this here. Don't bring up conflict among yourself and other coworkers, and instead focus on the motivation to keep up with the great work of others, and the ways in which coworkers may be a great support network in helping to push you to new successes.

4: When is it okay to socialize with coworkers?

Answer:

This question has two extreme answers (all the time, or never), and your interviewer, in most cases, will want to see that you fall somewhere in the middle. It's important to establish solid relationships with your coworkers, but never at the expense of getting work done. Ideally, relationship-building can happen with exercises of teamwork and special projects, as well as in the break room.

5: Tell me about a time when a major change was made at your last job, and how you handled it.

Answer:

Provide a set-up for the situation including the old system, what the change was, how it was implemented, and the results of the change, and include how you felt about each step of the way. Be sure that your initial thoughts on the old system are neutral, and that your excitement level grows with each step of the new change, as an interviewer will be pleased to see your adaptability.

6: When delegating tasks, how do you choose which tasks go to which team members?

Answer:

The interviewer is looking to gain insight into your thought process with this question, so be sure to offer thorough reasoning behind your choice. Explain that you delegate tasks based on each individual's personal strengths, or that you look at how many other projects each person is working on at the time, in order to create the best fit possible.

7: Tell me about a time when you had to stand up for something you believed strongly about to coworkers or a supervisor.

Answer:

While it may be difficult to explain a situation of conflict to an interviewer, this is a great opportunity to display your passions and convictions, and your dedication to your beliefs. Explain not just the situation to the interviewer, but also elaborate on why it was so important to you to stand up for the issue, and how your coworker or supervisor responded to you afterward – were they more respectful? Unreceptive? Open-minded? Apologetic?

8: Tell me about a time when you helped someone finish their work, even though it wasn't "your job."

Answer:

Though you may be frustrated when required to pick up someone else's slack, it's important that you remain positive about lending a hand. The interviewer will be looking to see if you're a team player, and by helping someone else finish a task that he or she couldn't manage alone, you show both your willingness to help the team succeed, and your own competence.

9: What are the challenges of working on a team? How do you handle this?

Answer:

There are many obvious challenges to working on a team, such as handling different perspectives, navigating individual schedules, or accommodating difficult workers. It's best to focus on one challenge, such as individual team members missing deadlines or failing to keep commitments, and then offer a solution that clearly addresses the problem. For example, you could organize weekly status meetings for your team to discuss progress, or assign shorter deadlines in order to keep the long-term deadline on schedule.

10: Do you value diversity in the workplace?

Answer:

Diversity is important in the workplace in order to foster an environment that is accepting, equalizing, and full of different perspectives and backgrounds. Be sure to show your awareness of these issues, and stress the importance of learning from others' experiences.

11: How would you handle a situation in which a coworker was not accepting of someone else's diversity?

Answer:

Explain that it is important to adhere to company policies regarding diversity, and that you would talk to the relevant supervisors or management team. When it is appropriate, it could also be best to talk to the coworker in question about the benefits of alternate perspectives – if you can handle the situation yourself, it's best not to bring resolvable issues to management.

12: Are you rewarded more from working on a team, or accomplishing a task on your own?

Answer:

It's best to show a balance between these two aspects – your employer wants to see that you're comfortable working on your own, and that you can complete tasks efficiently and well without assistance. However, it's also important for your employer to see that you can be a team player, and that you understand the value that multiple perspectives and efforts can bring to a project.

13: Tell me about a time when you didn't meet a deadline.

Answer:

Ideally, this hasn't happened – but if it has, make sure you use a minor example to illustrate the situation, emphasize how long ago it happened, and be sure that you did as much as you could to ensure that the deadline was met. Additionally, be sure to include what you learned about managing time better or prioritizing tasks in order to meet all future deadlines.

14: How do you eliminate distractions while working?

Answer:

With the increase of technology and the ease of communication, new distractions arise every day. Your interviewer will want to see that you are still able to focus on work, and that your productivity has not been affected, by an example showing a routine you employ in order to stay on task.

15: Tell me about a time when you worked in a position with a weekly or monthly quota to meet. How often were you successful?

Answer:

Your numbers will speak for themselves, and you must answer this question honestly. If you were regularly met your quotas, be sure to highlight this in a confident manner and don't be shy in pointing out your strengths in this area. If your statistics are less than stellar, try to point out trends in which they increased toward the end of your employment, and show reflection as to ways you can improve in the future.

16: Tell me about a time when you met a tough deadline, and how you were able to complete it.

Answer:

Explain how you were able to prioritize tasks, or to delegate portions of an assignments to other team members, in order to deal with a tough deadline. It may be beneficial to specify why the deadline was tough – make sure it's clear that it was not a result of procrastination on your part. Finally, explain how you were able to successfully meet the deadline, and what it took to get there in the end.

17: How do you stay organized when you have multiple projects on your plate?

Answer:

The interviewer will be looking to see that you can manage your time and work well – and being able to handle multiple projects at once, and still giving each the attention it deserves, is a great mark of a worker's competence and efficiency. Go through a typical process of goal-setting and prioritizing, and explain the steps of these to the interviewer, so he or she can see how well you manage time.

18: How much time during your work day do you spend on "auto-pilot?"

Answer:

While you may wonder if the employer is looking to see how efficient you are with this question (for example, so good at your job that you don't have to think about it), but in almost every case, the employer wants to see that you're constantly thinking, analyzing, and processing what's going on in the workplace. Even if things are running smoothly, there's usually an opportunity somewhere to make things more efficient or to increase sales or productivity. Stress your dedication to ongoing development, and convey that being on "auto-pilot" is not conducive to that type of success.

19: How do you handle deadlines?

Answer:

The most important part of handling tough deadlines is to

prioritize tasks and set goals for completion, as well as to delegate or eliminate unnecessary work. Lead the interviewer through a general scenario, and display your competency through your ability to organize and set priorities, and most importantly, remain calm.

20: Tell me about your personal problem-solving process.

Answer:

Your personal problem-solving process should include outlining the problem, coming up with possible ways to fix the problem, and setting a clear action plan that leads to resolution. Keep your answer brief and organized, and explain the steps in a concise, calm manner that shows you are level-headed even under stress.

21: What sort of things at work can make you stressed?

Answer:

As it's best to stay away from negatives, keep this answer brief and simple. While answering that nothing at work makes you stressed will not be very believable to the interviewer, keep your answer to one generic principle such as when members of a team don't keep their commitments, and then focus on a solution you generally employ to tackle that stress, such as having weekly status meetings or intermittent deadlines along the course of a project.

22: What do you look like when you are stressed about something? How do you solve it?

Answer:

This is a trick question – your interviewer wants to hear that you don't look any different when you're stressed, and that you don't allow negative emotions to interfere with your productivity. As far as how you solve your stress, it's best if you have a simple solution mastered, such as simply taking deep breaths and counting to 10 to bring yourself back to the task at hand.

23: Can you multi-task?

Answer:

Some people can, and some people can't. The most important part of multi-tasking is to keep a clear head at all times about what needs to be done, and what priority each task falls under. Explain how you evaluate tasks to determine priority, and how you manage your time in order to ensure that all are completed efficiently.

24: How many hours per week do you work?

Answer:

Many people get tricked by this question, thinking that answering more hours is better – however, this may cause an employer to wonder why you have to work so many hours in order to get the work done that other people can do in a shorter amount of time. Give a fair estimate of hours that it should take you to complete a job, and explain that you are also willing to work extra whenever needed.

25: How many times per day do you check your email?

Answer:

While an employer wants to see that you are plugged into modern technology, it is also important that the number of times you check your email per day is relatively low – perhaps two to three times per day (dependent on the specific field you're in). Checking email is often a great distraction in the workplace, and while it is important to remain connected, much correspondence can simply be handled together in the morning and afternoon.

26: Tell me about a time when you worked additional hours to finish a project.

Answer:

It's important for your employer to see that you are dedicated to your work, and willing to put in extra hours when required or when a job calls for it. However, be careful when explaining why you were called to work additional hours – for instance, did you have to stay late because you set goals poorly earlier in the process? Or on a more positive note, were you working additional hours because a client requested for a deadline to be moved up on short notice? Stress your competence and willingness to give 110% every time.

27: Tell me about a time when your performance exceeded the duties and requirements of your job.

Answer:

If you're a great candidate for the position, this should be an

easy question to answer – choose a time when you truly went above and beyond the call of duty, and put in additional work or voluntarily took on new responsib-ilities. Remain humble, and express gratitude for the learning opportunity, as well as confidence in your ability
to give a repeat performance.

28: What is your driving attitude about work?
Answer:
There are many possible good answers to this question, and the interviewer primarily wants to see that you have a great passion for the job and that you will remain motivated in your career if hired. Some specific driving forces behind your success may include hard work, opportunity, growth potential, or success.

29: Do you take work home with you?
Answer:
It is important to first clarify that you are always willing to take work home when necessary, but you want to emphasize as well that it has not been an issue for you in the past. Highlight skills such as time management, goal-setting, and multi-tasking, which can all ensure that work is completed at work.

30: Describe a typical work day to me.
Answer:
There are several important components in your typical work day, and an interviewer may derive meaning from any or all of

them, as well as from your ability to systematically lead him or her through the day. Start at the beginning of your day and proceed chronologically, making sure to emphasize steady productivity, time for review, goal-setting, and prioritizing, as well as some additional time to account for unexpected things that may arise.

31: Tell me about a time when you went out of your way at your previous job.

Answer:

Here it is best to use a specific example of the situation that required you to go out of your way, what your specific position would have required that you did, and how you went above that. Use concrete details, and be sure to include the results, as well as reflection on what you learned in the process.

32: Are you open to receiving feedback and criticisms on your job performance, and adjusting as necessary?

Answer:

This question has a pretty clear answer – yes – but you'll need to display a knowledge as to why this is important. Receiving feedback and criticism is one thing, but the most important part of that process is to then implement it into your daily work. Keep a good attitude, and express that you always appreciate constructive feedback.

33: What inspires you?

Answer:

You may find inspiration in nature, reading success stories, or mastering a difficult task, but it's important that your inspiration is positively-based and that you're able to listen and tune into it when it appears. Keep this answer generally based in the professional world, but where applicable, it may stretch a bit into creative exercises in your personal life that, in turn, help you in achieving career objectives.

34: How do you inspire others?

Answer:

This may be a difficult question, as it is often hard to discern the effects of inspiration in others. Instead of offering a specific example of a time when you inspired someone, focus on general principles such as leading by example that you employ in your professional life. If possible, relate this to a quality that someone who inspired you possessed, and discuss the way you have modified or modeled it in your own work.

35: How do you make decisions?

Answer:

This is a great opportunity for you to wow your interviewer with your decisiveness, confidence, and organizational skills. Make sure that you outline a process for decision-making, and that you stress the importance of weighing your options, as well as in trusting intuition. If you answer this question skillfully and with ease, your interviewer will trust in your capability as a worker.

36: What are the most difficult decisions for you to make?

Answer:

Explain your relationship to decision-making, and a general synopsis of the process you take in making choices. If there is a particular type of decision that you often struggle with, such as those that involve other people, make sure to explain why that type of decision is tough for you, and how you are currently engaged in improving your skills.

37: When making a tough decision, how do you gather information?

Answer:

If you're making a tough choice, it's best to gather information from as many sources as possible. Lead the interviewer through your process of taking information from people in different areas, starting first with advice from experts in your field, feedback from coworkers or other clients, and by looking analytically at your own past experiences.

38: Tell me about a decision you made that did not turn out well.

Answer:

Honesty and transparency are great values that your interviewer will appreciate – outline the choice you made, why you made it, the results of your poor decision – and finally (and most importantly!) what you learned from the decision. Give the interviewer reason to trust that you wouldn't make a decision like that again in the future.

39: Are you able to make decisions quickly?

Answer:

You may be able to make decisions quickly, but be sure to communicate your skill in making sound, thorough decisions as well. Discuss the importance of making a decision quickly, and how you do so, as well as the necessity for each decision to first be well-informed.

40: Ten years ago, what were your career goals?

Answer:

In reflecting back to what your career goals were ten years ago, it's important to show the ways in which you've made progress in that time. Draw distinct links between specific objectives that you've achieved, and speak candidly about how it felt to reach those goals. Remain positive, upbeat, and growth-oriented, even if you haven't yet achieved all of the goals you set out to reach.

41: Tell me about a weakness you used to have, and how you changed it.

Answer:

Choose a non-professional weakness that you used to have, and outline the process you went through in order to grow past it. Explain the weakness itself, why it was problematic, the action steps you planned, how you achieved them, and the end result.

42: Tell me about your goal-setting process.

Answer:

When describing your goal-setting process, clearly outline the way that you create an outline for yourself. It may be helpful to offer an example of a particular goal you've set in the past, and use this as a starting point to guide the way you created action steps, check-in points, and how the goal was eventually achieved.

43: Tell me about a time when you solved a problem by creating actionable steps to follow.

Answer:

This question will help the interviewer to see how you talented you are in outlining, problem resolution, and goal-setting. Explain thoroughly the procedure of outlining the problem, establishing steps to take, and then how you followed the steps (such as through check-in points along the way, or intermediary goals).

44: Where do you see yourself five years from now?

Answer:

Have some idea of where you would like to have advanced to in the position you're applying for, over the next several years. Make sure that your future plans line up with you still working for the company, and stay positive about potential advancement. Focus on future opportunities, and what you're looking forward to – but make sure your reasons for advancement are admirable, such as greater experience and the chance to learn, rather than simply being out for a higher salary.

45: When in a position, do you look for opportunities to promote?

Answer:

There's a fine balance in this question – you want to show the interviewer that you have initiative and motivation to advance in your career, but not at the expense of appearing opportunistic or selfishly-motivated. Explain that you are always open to growth opportunities, and very willing to take on new responsibilities as your career advances.

46: On a scale of 1 to 10, how successful has your life been?

Answer:

Though you may still have a long list of goals to achieve, it's important to keep this answer positively-focused. Choose a high number between 7 and 9, and explain that you feel your life has been largely successful and satisfactory as a result of several specific achievements or experiences. Don't go as high as a 10, as the interviewer may not believe your response or in your ability to reason critically.

47: What is your greatest goal in life?

Answer:

It's okay for this answer to stray a bit into your personal life, but best if you can keep it professionally-focused. While specific goals are great, if your personal goal doesn't match up exactly with one of the company's objectives, you're better off keeping your goal a little more generic and encompassing, such as "success in my career" or "leading a happy and fulfilling life." Keep your answer brief, and show a decisive nature – most importantly, make it clear that you've already thought about this question and know what you want.

48: Tell me about a time when you set a goal in your personal life and achieved it.

Answer:

The interviewer can see that you excel at setting goals in your professional life, but he or she also wants to know that you are consistent in your life and capable of setting goals outside of the office as well. Use an example such as making a goal to eat more healthily or to drink more water, and discuss what steps you outlined to achieve your goal, the process of taking action, and the final results as well.

49: What is your greatest goal in your career?

Answer:

Have a very specific goal of something you want to achieve in your career in mind, and be sure that it's something the position clearly puts you in line to accomplish. Offer the goal as well as your plans to get there, and emphasize clear ways in which this position will be an opportunity to work toward the goal.

50: Tell me about a time when you achieved a goal.

Answer:

Start out with how you set the goal, and why you chose it. Then, take the interviewer through the process of outlining the goal, taking steps to achieve it, the outcome, and finally, how you felt after achieving it or recognition you received. The most important part of this question includes the planning and implementation of strategies, so focus most of your time on explaining these aspects. However, the preliminary decisions and end results are also important, so make sure to include them as well.

51: What areas of your work would you still like to improve in? What are your plans to do this?
Answer:
While you may not want the interviewer to focus on things you could improve on, it's important to be self-aware of your own growth opportunities. More importantly, you can impress an interviewer by having specific goals and actions outlined in order to facilitate your growth, even if your area of improvement is something as simple as increasing sales or finding new ways to create greater efficiency.

And Finally Good Luck!

INDEX

Window Server 2008 R2

Basics of Windows Server 2008 R2

Active Directory Services Installation and Administration

machine as a Domain Controller. Which command you will type to do so?

18: Which command would you use to add or remove roles in Windows Server 2008 R2 Server Core?

19: You are the Administrator of a company named DATACORP.COM. It contains Windows Server 2008 R2 promoted as a Domain Controller and configured as Global Catalog (GC) which also holds all five operation master roles. You have also deployed another Domain Controller in your domain. However, it is not configured as GC. What Flexible Single Master Operations (FSMO) Role should you transfer to the non-GC domain controller?

20: What are the pre-requisites to add a computer to the domain?

21: What is pre-staging?

22: How many types of Operation Master Roles are there in a forest?

23: How many types of Active Directory partitions are there?

24: In which case you should enable Universal Group Membership Caching (UGMC) in a site?

25: How many Forest Functional Levels does Windows Server 2008 R2 have?

26: Which Operation Master role is responsible for time synchronization and password changing?

27: What do you understand by the term Certificate Revocation?

28: What is the function of Infrastructure Master Role?

29: What is symmetric encryption?

30: What is Asymmetric encryption?

31: What do you understand by single sign on (SSO)?

32: What do you understand by Network Device Enrollment Service (NDES)?

33: What is the difference between trusted domain and trusting domain?

34: What is a pre-shared key?

35: What is Integrated Windows Authentication?

36: What are bridgehead servers?

37: What is the function of Key Recovery Agent (KRA)?

38: What is Client Certificate Authentication method?

39: What is Selective Authentication?

40: What is a trust?

41: What are the prerequisites for deploying AD FS (Active Directory Federation Services)?

42: What is the use of Active Directory Recycle Bin in Windows Server 2008 R2?

43: What is Distinguished Name?

44: What is Auto Enrollment?

45: What are the two types of Replication Transport Protocols in Active Directory Sites and Services snap-in?

46: What is a Global Catalog Server?

47: What is the function of Schema Master?

48: Which protocol is used by AD LDS?

49: What are the core elements of the AD CS infrastructure?

50: What is Certificate Revocation List (CRL)?

51: Describe the concept of Administrator role separation.

52: Which FSMO roles you can transfer from a domain

controller to another domain controller in a different domain in a forest?

53: In which condition you can replicate SYSVOL by using DFS-R within that domain?

54: What is Intersite replication?

55: What is Intrasite replication?

56: What should be the minimum Forest and Domain Functional Level for deploying RODC?

57: Name the built-in Data Collector Sets in Windows Server 2008 R2.

58: What is Data Collector Set?

59: What is the difference between Enterprise CA and Standalone CA?

60: Which Server Roles are supported by Windows Server 2008 R2 Server Core?

61: What do you understand by RODC credential caching?

62: Where does Active Directory store its Database?

63: What do you understand by the process Offline Domain Join?

64: What are Site Link Bridges?

65: Describe the features provided by Windows Server2008 R2 domain functional level.

66: How can you create application partitions for AD LDS instances?

Active Directory Users Groups and Computers

67: A user logs on to a Domain using User1@Datacorp.com credentials. What is the other credential method of logging on to a Domain?

68: You are an Administrator in a company. You have three sites, Sydney, Dallas and New Delhi. CEO of the organization has decided to dissolve Dallas branch. When you attempt to remove all OUs created for Dallas site it responds as: The object is protected from accidental deletion. What will you do to delete this Organizational Unit (OU)?

69: You are the administrator of a company named DATACORP.COM. You hired a tech support engineer so that you can delegate some administrative task of adding users, creating users and resetting user passwords to him. Which tool or feature will you use to do so?

70: What is an Organizational Unit (OU)?

71: You are the administrator of a company named DATACORP.COM. When you initiated Active Directory Users and Computers snap-in, you found that one of the users' icons in Users container has a small down arrow. What does it mean?

72: How many scopes does a domain group have?

73: What is secondary logon?

74: What is UPN suffix?

75: What is the difference between local users and domain users?

76: Why do you create a shadow group?

77: By default, members of which group can create Password Setting Objects (PSOs)?

78: What type of Active Directory objects a Universal Group can contain?

79: In which environment should you use Distribution groups?

DHCP

80: What is the purpose of creating reservations in DHCP?

81: When does a client obtain an IP address of 169.254.0.0/16 range?

82: What is a Super Scope?

83: When does a DHCP client request DHCP server for IP address renewal?

84: What is the default lease duration for which an IP address is assigned to a client computer by the DHCP server?

85: Describe the process of DORA.

86: What is the function of DHCP relay agent?

87: What do you understand by exclusions in DHCP?

88: When you configure ICS what IP address is assigned to the internal network adapter?

89: What is the difference between DHCP and DHCPv6?

IP Addressing

90: What is the loopback address in IPv6?

91: How many bits are there in an IPv6 address?

92: What are Global addresses in IPv6?

93: What is Link Local Multicast Name Resolution (LLMNR) method?

94: Which protocol replaces the Address Resolution Protocol (ARP) in IPv6?

95: Which protocol connects IPv6 hosts and routers over IPv4 networks?

96: What are the different types of IPv6 transition strategies?

Network and Application Infrastructure

97: What is a RADIUS Server?

98: Which protocol is used for smart card authentication?

99: What is Distributed File System (DFS)?

100: Name the types of VPN tunneling protocol.

101: What are the prerequisites for deploying Windows Deployment Services (WDS)?

102: What is Hyper-V or Hypervisor?

103: Which TCP port is used to initiate RDP connections to terminal servers?

104: What do you understand by the term DFS namespace?

105: Why Windows Server Update Services (WSUS) server is used?

106: What do you understand by printer pooling?

107: How many maximum concurrent Remote Desktop sessions can be initiated on a computer running Windows Server 2008 R2?

108: What is the changed name of Terminal Services in Windows Server 2008 R2?

109: In a RADIUS oriented environment, who acts as a radius client?

110: What are the major Distributed File System (DFS) elements?

111: Which port is used by Remote Desktop Gateway to communicate with clients over SSL?

112: What is the benefit of FTPS over FTP?

113: Which command is used to initiate IIS 7.5 Manager?

114: Which streaming protocol is used by Windows media

services?

115: What are the system requirements for deploying Hyper-V in Windows Server 2008 R2?

116: How many logical cores does a single instance and single Virtual Machine instance of Windows Server 2008 R2 support?

Security

117: You are the Administrator of a company. For security reason management decided that a particular user must not logon after 4.00 p.m. What appropriate action will you take?

118: You have created a shared folder in a file server and you want that Marketing group can access the shared folder but Accounts group cannot. What will you do?

119: Your Company undertakes a new project and you want to give access to your domain partner on your file server to a specific folder. What type of group will you create so that they can access that folder?

120: What is the difference between authentication and authorization?

121: Describe the benefits provided by the SSL (Secure Sockets Layer).

122: What do you understand by Network Level Authentication?

123: What do you understand by the term Kerberos authentication?

124: Why do we need DRA?

125: What is Transport Layer Security (TLS)?

126: What is Access Control List (ACL)?

127: What is Domain Isolation Policy?

128: What is BitLocker Drive Encryption?

Name Resolution in Windows Server 2008 R2

129: You have established a domain/client network infrastructure using Windows Server 2008 R2 and have named the domain as DATACORP.COM. What will be the NetBIOS name of the domain?

130: You are an Administrator of DATACORP.COM. When you try to add a client computer to DATACORP.COM domain it gives an error saying: An Active Directory Domain Controller for the domain DATACORP.COM could not be contacted. How will you resolve this problem?

131: In IP v4 DNS representation of host records is A. What is the representation of host records in IP v6?

132: What are Root Hints?

133: Why do we need to configure conditional forwarders?

134: You are the administrator of a company named DATACORP.COM that has two sites, Dallas and Sydney. Both sites have DNS Servers. Sites are connected via 256 Kbps WAN link. To save your bandwidth and for better query resolution, you created a stub zone for Sydney site in Dallas site but when you attempt to reload the zone or transfer from master it gives an error- Unable to transfer from master. What could be the real cause?

135: Why do you need to configure scavenging and aging on a DNS server?

136: When do we need to configure Forwarders?

137: What do you understand by DNS recursion?

138: What types of records does a stub zone contain?

139: In which scenario we can use Caching Only DNS Server?

140: Which resource records are used to resolve queries for Exchange Server?

141: Describe the process of how Secondary DNS server receives DNS records from Master DNS server.

142: What is the use of stub zone?

143: What is Active Directory integrated zone?

144: What do you understand by DNS suffix?

145: What do you understand by the Glue Record?

146: What are Pointer (PTR) records?

147: What is NetBIOS name resolution?

148: What is GlobalNames Zone?

149: Name the scopes available for DNS Zone replication in Active Directory infrastructure.

150: What are Name Servers?

151: What is the use of LMhosts file?

152: Why should you configure alternate DNS server address?

153: What are the DNS zone transfer options available in the Zone Transfers tab in Windows Server 2008 R2?

154: What is the newly added feature in Windows Server 2008 R2 which allows client computers to verify the authenticity of the DNS record?

155: What is the use of cache.dns file and where it is found?

156: What is BIND in DNS?

157: What is the difference between Forward Lookup and Reverse Lookup Zone?

158: In which condition can we store a DNS zone in Active Directory?

Disk Management and Storage

159: What is the difference between basic disk and dynamic disk?

160: What is the difference between Network Attached Storage (NAS) and Direct Attached Storage (DAS)?

161: What do you understand by Network Load Balancing Cluster?

162: What is SMB?

163: Why offline files are important?

164: What are RAID volumes?

165: What is Network File System (NFS)?

166: What is Cluster Shared Volumes (CSV)?

167: Why do we need to configure Disk quota?

168: What is the difference between Hard Quota and Soft Quota?

169: What is a Witness Disk?

170: Which editions of Windows Sever 2008 R2 support failover clustering?

Backup and Restore

171: What is Volume Shadow Copy?

172: What is Bare Metal restore?

173 What is the command line tool used to performing an Active Directory authoritative restore?

174: How can you perform a Non-Authoritative Restore?

175: What is the main benefit of restoring Active Directory using Installation from Media (IFM) process?

Scripting

176: As an administrator of DATACORP.COM you need to create 200 domain user accounts. How will you complete the task with least administrative overhead?

177: Which command is used to manage SYSVOL replication when Forest Functional Level is Windows Server 2008 R2?

178: Which command-line utility is used to perform initial configuration of WDS (Windows Deployment Services) Server in Windows Server 2008 R2?

179: Which command is used to enable Active Directory Recycle Bin feature in Windows Server 2008 R2?

180: What does OOBE command do?

181: Which command line tool is used to troubleshoot DNS server?

182: Through which command we can convert a Security Policy into a Group Policy Object (GPO)?

183: Which command is used to update Group Policy settings on a client computer?

184: Which command is used to manage DNS server from command line?

185: Which command is used to renew an IP address assigned by DHCP server?

186: Which command you must use to deploy Read Only Domain Controller (RODC)?

187: Why do we initiate ipconfig /flushdns command?

188: What command is used to add client computers to a specific DHCP User Class?

189: Which command line utility is used to administer Windows SharePoint Services?

190: What is Windows PowerShell?

Group Policy Objects

191: What are Starter GPOs?

192: Being an Administrator of DATACORP.COM you have configured a GPO named DesktopLock that has following settings: You want to link it to an OU named DatacorpUsers which also contains a child OU named Executives. What will you do to prevent Executives OU from inheriting settings from DesktopLock GPO?

193: You are an administrator at DATACORP.COM. For security reasons, you want that users cannot plug any USB or removable devices to the computers. What appropriate action you should take to do so?

194: In which condition you are required to configure Loopback Policy Processing?

195: You want to install Microsoft Word 2007 on all your client computers in the network. How would you accomplish the task with least administrative overhead?

196: What are fine grained policies in Windows Server 2008 R2?

197: Name the two built-in GPOs that are by default created when AD DS is installed.

198: What is the difference between Default Domain Policy and Default Domain Controller Policy?

199: What are the two ways of deploying software through group policies?

200: What is the difference between assigning an application and publishing an application in Group Policy?

HR Questions

1: How would you handle a negative coworker?

2: What would you do if you witnessed a coworker surfing the web, reading a book, etc, wasting company time?

3: How do you handle competition among yourself and other employees?

4: When is it okay to socialize with coworkers?

5: Tell me about a time when a major change was made at your last job, and how you handled it.

6: When delegating tasks, how do you choose which tasks go to which team members?

7: Tell me about a time when you had to stand up for something you believed strongly about to coworkers or a supervisor.

8: Tell me about a time when you helped someone finish their work, even though it wasn't "your job."

9: What are the challenges of working on a team? How do you handle this?

10: Do you value diversity in the workplace?

11: How would you handle a situation in which a coworker was not accepting of someone else's diversity?

12: Are you rewarded more from working on a team, or accomplishing a task on your own?

13: Tell me about a time when you didn't meet a deadline.

14: How do you eliminate distractions while working?

15: Tell me about a time when you worked in a position with a weekly or monthly quota to meet. How often were you successful?

16: Tell me about a time when you met a tough deadline, and how you were able to complete it.

17: How do you stay organized when you have multiple projects on your plate?

18: How much time during your work day do you spend on "auto-pilot?"

19: How do you handle deadlines?

20: Tell me about your personal problem-solving process.

21: What sort of things at work can make you stressed?

22: What do you look like when you are stressed about something? How do you solve it?

23: Can you multi-task?

24: How many hours per week do you work?

25: How many times per day do you check your email?

26: Tell me about a time when you worked additional hours to finish a project.

27: Tell me about a time when your performance exceeded the duties and requirements of your job.

28: What is your driving attitude about work?

29: Do you take work home with you?

30: Describe a typical work day to me.

31: Tell me about a time when you went out of your way at your previous job.

32: Are you open to receiving feedback and criticisms on your job performance, and adjusting as necessary?

33: What inspires you?

34: How do you inspire others?

35: How do you make decisions?

36: What are the most difficult decisions for you to make?

37: When making a tough decision, how do you gather information?

38: Tell me about a decision you made that did not turn out well.

39: Are you able to make decisions quickly?

40: Ten years ago, what were your career goals?

41: Tell me about a weakness you used to have, and how you changed it.

42: Tell me about your goal-setting process.

43: Tell me about a time when you solved a problem by creating actionable steps to follow.

44: Where do you see yourself five years from now?

45: When in a position, do you look for opportunities to promote?

46: On a scale of 1 to 10, how successful has your life been?

47: What is your greatest goal in life?

48: Tell me about a time when you set a goal in your personal life and achieved it.

49: What is your greatest goal in your career?

50: Tell me about a time when you achieved a goal.

51: What areas of your work would you still like to improve in? What are your plans to do this?

Some of the following titles might also be handy:

1. .NET Interview Questions You'll Most Likely Be Asked

2. 200 Interview Questions You'll Most Likely Be Asked

3. Access VBA Programming Interview Questions You'll Most Likely Be Asked

4. Adobe ColdFusion Interview Questions You'll Most Likely Be Asked

5. Advanced JAVA Interview Questions You'll Most Likely Be Asked

6. AJAX Interview Questions You'll Most Likely Be Asked

7. Algorithms Interview Questions You'll Most Likely Be Asked

8. Android Development Interview Questions You'll Most Likely Be Asked

9. Ant & Maven Interview Questions You'll Most Likely Be Asked

10. Apache Web Server Interview Questions You'll Most Likely Be Asked

11. ASP.NET Interview Questions You'll Most Likely Be Asked

12. Automated Software Testing Interview Questions You'll Most Likely Be Asked

13. Base SAS Interview Questions You'll Most Likely Be Asked

14. BEA WebLogic Server Interview Questions You'll Most Likely Be Asked

15. C & C++ Interview Questions You'll Most Likely Be Asked

16. C# Interview Questions You'll Most Likely Be Asked

17. C++ Internals Interview Questions You'll Most Likely Be Asked

18. CCNA Interview Questions You'll Most Likely Be Asked

19. Cloud Computing Interview Questions You'll Most Likely Be Asked

20. Computer Architecture Interview Questions You'll Most Likely Be Asked

21. Core JAVA Interview Questions You'll Most Likely Be Asked

22. Data Structures & Algorithms Interview Questions You'll Most Likely Be Asked

23. Data WareHousing Interview Questions You'll Most Likely Be Asked

24. EJB 3.0 Interview Questions You'll Most Likely Be Asked

25. Entity Framework Interview Questions You'll Most Likely Be Asked

26. Fedora & RHEL Interview Questions You'll Most Likely Be Asked

27. GNU Development Interview Questions You'll Most Likely Be Asked

28. Hibernate, Spring & Struts Interview Questions You'll Most Likely Be Asked

29. HTML, XHTML and CSS Interview Questions You'll Most Likely Be Asked

30. HTML5 Interview Questions You'll Most Likely Be Asked

31. IBM WebSphere Application Server Interview Questions You'll Most Likely Be Asked

32. iOS SDK Interview Questions You'll Most Likely Be Asked

33. Java / J2EE Design Patterns Interview Questions You'll Most Likely Be Asked

34. Java / J2EE Interview Questions You'll Most Likely Be Asked

35. Java Messaging Service Interview Questions You'll Most Likely Be Asked

36. JavaScript Interview Questions You'll Most Likely Be Asked

37. JavaServer Faces Interview Questions You'll Most Likely Be Asked

38. JDBC Interview Questions You'll Most Likely Be Asked

39. jQuery Interview Questions You'll Most Likely Be Asked

40. JSP-Servlet Interview Questions You'll Most Likely Be Asked

41. JUnit Interview Questions You'll Most Likely Be Asked

42. Linux Commands Interview Questions You'll Most Likely Be Asked

43. Linux Interview Questions You'll Most Likely Be Asked

44. Linux System Administrator Interview Questions You'll Most Likely Be Asked

45. Mac OS X Lion Interview Questions You'll Most Likely Be Asked

46. Mac OS X Snow Leopard Interview Questions You'll Most Likely Be Asked

47. Microsoft Access Interview Questions You'll Most Likely Be Asked

48. Microsoft Excel Interview Questions You'll Most Likely Be Asked

49. Microsoft Powerpoint Interview Questions You'll Most Likely Be Asked

50. Microsoft Word Interview Questions You'll Most Likely Be Asked

51. MySQL Interview Questions You'll Most Likely Be Asked

52. NetSuite Interview Questions You'll Most Likely Be Asked

53. Networking Interview Questions You'll Most Likely Be Asked

54. OOPS Interview Questions You'll Most Likely Be Asked

55. Oracle DBA Interview Questions You'll Most Likely Be Asked

56. Oracle E-Business Suite Interview Questions You'll Most Likely Be Asked

57. ORACLE PL/SQL Interview Questions You'll Most Likely Be Asked

58. Perl Interview Questions You'll Most Likely Be Asked

59. PHP Interview Questions You'll Most Likely Be Asked

60. PMP Interview Questions You'll Most Likely Be Asked

61. Python Interview Questions You'll Most Likely Be Asked

62. RESTful JAVA Web Services Interview Questions You'll Most Likely Be Asked

63. Ruby Interview Questions You'll Most Likely Be Asked

64. Ruby on Rails Interview Questions You'll Most Likely Be Asked

65. SAP ABAP Interview Questions You'll Most Likely Be Asked

66. Selenium Testing Tools Interview Questions You'll Most Likely Be Asked

67. Silverlight Interview Questions You'll Most Likely Be Asked

68. Software Repositories Interview Questions You'll Most Likely Be Asked

69. Software Testing Interview Questions You'll Most Likely Be Asked

70. SQL Server Interview Questions You'll Most Likely Be Asked

71. Tomcat Interview Questions You'll Most Likely Be Asked

72. UML Interview Questions You'll Most Likely Be Asked

73. Unix Interview Questions You'll Most Likely Be Asked

74. UNIX Shell Programming Interview Questions You'll Most Likely Be Asked

75. VB.NET Interview Questions You'll Most Likely Be Asked

76. XLXP, XSLT, XPath, XForms & XQuery Interview Questions You'll Most Likely Be Asked

77. XML Interview Questions You'll Most Likely Be Asked

For complete list visit

www.vibrantpublishers.com

NOTES

www.ingramcontent.com/pod-product-compliance
Lightning Source LLC
Chambersburg PA
CBHW071215050326
40689CB00011B/2333